Words *for* Work

HS PRESS

ISBN: 979-8-88737-090-3
Cover Image: paseven/Shutterstock.com
AKaiser/Shutterstock.com
alex74/Shutterstock.com
Nata_Alhontess/Shutterstock.com

Words *for* Work

EL CANTARE

Ryuho Okawa

HS PRESS

Contents

Words for Work

Words for Work

$$\textcircled{1}$$

To work—that is the condition
for living in this world.

(2)

Work must be beneficial and

useful to others.

③

If work was fun like going to

an amusement park,

the company could charge

employees an admission fee.

Therefore, work cannot be
as enjoyable as having fun
at Disneyland.

(5)

There is no one

new to the job

who has not been scolded.

(6)

Whether you are a high school graduate or a university graduate, the knowledge you studied at school will not help you. You will have to start from the bottom.

All new employees are
a burden everywhere and are
treated like idiots.

(8)

If new employees who have just
come out of university think
they are superior like gods,
they will be treated poorly like
dirt even by colleagues who
started a year before them.

(9)

It takes at least three years to understand what your senior colleagues are saying without an interpreter.

(10)

If you brag about your education before learning the "ABCs" of the job, you are likely to become deadwood in the company.

11

When you transfer to a new department, you will have to beg for instructions from junior staff and those younger than you.

(12)

You cannot understand the advice and guidance of those who have twenty years of experience unless you have been with the company for three years.

(13)

When one new hire comes in,
one experienced worker will be
too distracted to get any work done.

So do not show off

what little you know or

talk back to your seniors.

15

To receive advice from others,

you must be humble.

This is a manner you should have.

16

First and foremost, master all
the basics of work in your office.

Until your third year of employment, your salary is "a loss" to the company.

(18)

When giving a task to a newbie,

give them written instructions.

Newbies, double-check the figures and details of the tasks given by your superiors.

(20)

Don't trust a boss who is quick to praise you. Most likely they are laughing behind your back.

(21)

Be cautious of academic elitist groups. Intelligence and school prestige hopelessly contradict.

(22)

Diligent bosses and honest superiors are the ones you should learn from and follow.

(23)

When you instruct a new employee,

think back to the unfair treatment

you received and be careful

not to do the same thing.

(24)

People who are highly competent but who tend to make enemies will not be given work that suits their abilities.

(25)

Don't try to be too familiar with

colleagues too soon.

Keep a certain distance and

be polite to them.

You must not point out

someone's shortcomings and

faults in front of others.

If you do, you'll create

a lifetime enemy.

(27)

Remember that others will never forget you criticizing, swearing, and bragging even during drinking or off-hours.

(28)

Where should the
"head of the table" sit and
which is the "VIP seat" in the car?
Know these things to have
good manners.

(29)

Boasting about your fluency
in another language is annoying
even at international trading
companies. Strive to work on
what you can improve instead.

(30)

Those who are smart but cannot
get promoted are not team
players two-thirds of the time.
Think about how to achieve
good results as a team.

(31)

Only a few selected elites will be
assigned to work that involves
decision-making or negotiation
with just three to five years of
experience under their belt.
So first, learn to complete desk
work with accuracy.

(32)

Being considerate and attentive

are conditions for success,

but what "hits the bull's eye"

is a job well done.

33

If you are not trusted by family or friends, you will not get ahead in your company.

It's a big mistake if you think you can fool others by pretending to be a good person only while on duty.

(35)

At work, you cannot get your way
by pretending or making excuses.
Sincerity in both public life and
private life is important.

(36)

Never underestimate a person

who is polite, gentle-mannered,

and well-spoken.

They are a few steps ahead of you.

Those who see the big picture
and can get work done efficiently
are the ones you should learn from.

(38)

Superiors who have learned
all the basics and accumulated
their own know-how of work are
the ones you should learn from
and follow.

Creative-minded people can come up with completely new solutions for work that have never been tried before.

Which would you do,

run away from a problem or

courageously face it?

Many people are watching

you objectively.

Don't be deceitful.

No one wants to work with liars.

(42)

Those who get together and
speak ill of others are immature.

43

Practice and rehearsal are important. But people who take too long to prepare generally lack talent.

People who can reply promptly with well-chosen words can be described as quick thinkers.

People who demand scripts and
project outlines for everything
have average or
less-than-average intellect.

If you cannot stand in another

person's position and think of

what you would do,

you cannot manage others.

If you are often told,

"Your work is slow,"

it is almost the same as being told,

"You won't get far in your career."

"Reporting, communicating,

and consulting" are

the foundation of work.

You need to report on the progress

of long-term projects regularly.

Women like men who are considerate, not ones who chase after them all the time.

(50)

A romantic relationship
in the office gone wrong will
ruin your reputation. Be aware
that it could get you transferred.

(51)

Exceptional are those who can keep important information confidential.

People who cannot keep
important information confidential
will not be assigned to
important sections.

(53)

Those who are making efforts to

go one step further every day

will not go unnoticed.

When a quick thinker becomes contemplative, it is a sign that they will soon be promoted.

(55)

If overtime increases

when that person comes in,

and work gets done faster

when that person leaves,

he is a toxic employee.

56

Those who watch what's going on without being deliberate are competent. Those who assume no one is watching them when they are being watched are incompetent.

You have one mouth and two ears.

Listen twice as much as you speak.

(58)

People who always want to be in

the spotlight are always disliked

by others.

People who are financially

irresponsible will have

this bad habit throughout life.

An inferiority complex often

expresses itself in flashy behavior.

(61)

People who constantly challenge

those who are smarter are digging

their own graves every day.

(62)

Being a good loser is a good trait.

A loss is a loss. A win is a win.

Keep going forward

steadily and calmly.

If you find deceitfulness in yourself,

make every effort to correct it.

Desire to have a noble attitude

toward life that even

your enemies would admire.

"The boughs that bear the most

hang the lowest."

The higher you rise in the ranks,

the humbler you should be.

Check and see if

you are not mistaking

your company's credibility

for your own credibility.

Knowledge is power.

Gain a deeper understanding of

nurturing love.

People who can humbly

take a scolding are the ones

who can grow.

Let there be stillness in motion.

Maintain a calm mind

when you are most busy.

When you push away water in

the tub, it flows back to you.

When you pull the water to you,

it flows away.

(71)

Have respect for people who
have achieved both happiness at
home and success at work.

(72)

Sometimes, we can

get through difficult situations by

apologizing a lot and

thanking a lot.

(73)

Having an affair is joyful yet

hellish at the same time.

At least, try to avoid going to

the Hell of the Bloody Pond

after death.

Strive to increase your income and

keep expenses to a minimum.

This principle of money applies to

both your life and your company.

(75)

Are you mixing up business

with personal matters?

As you rise in the ranks,

you will have to be more cautious

of your actions.

A fair and selfless attitude is

akin to enlightenment.

The expression on your face

will show your personality.

Is it getting better as you age?

(78)

Can you capture people's hearts with a short speech? There is no end to the road to mastery.

Keep on working like a

diligent and honest craftsman.

You will unexpectedly achieve

great success.

(80)

New knowledge and meditation
are the two major sources of
good ideas.

(81)

When you are over fifty,

make friends with those who are

thirty years younger than you.

$$\textcircled{82}$$

What you are studying now

will create the work you will do

ten years later.

(83)

The greater success

you achieve in your work,

the stronger enemies

you will face.

Like sandpaper, they will help

polish your soul.

(84)

The full responsibility for crisis
management always lies with
the top executive.

The purpose of a divisional structure in a company is to nurture tomorrow's managers, not to secure seats for incompetent employees.

(86)

You cannot build a big company

if you are ignorant of

international affairs.

Learning and

practicing a foreign language

will prevent you from going senile

and will broaden your horizons.

(88)

Raising children is like

frying eggs —

neither too burnt nor too raw.

Training a successor of a company

is the most difficult task.

It's important to have

several people in mind and

to also weed out the

less qualified candidates.

(90)

You must not make a dishonest

person the next leader.

(91)

As a manager, always keep in mind
the Buddha's teachings of "Birth,
Aging, Illness, and Death," and
"The Impermanence of All Things."

The abilities of managers will be

revealed in how far they can read

into the future and move

their pawns strategically.

(93)

The traditional spirit of selfless

devotion to one's feudal lord

is not out-of-date.

Just replace "feudal lord"

with *society* or *country* and the

spirit lives on today.

When your love for your family

and your love for your company

start to clash, it means you must

take greater responsibility

in your position or your company

has a greater influence

on the public.

It is difficult to decide when to

resign from your position;

you must always have an

objective view of yourself and

the trend of the times.

When worse comes to worst,
your business will fall into the
hands of others or go bankrupt.
Brace yourself and be prepared
to accept it.

(97)

What is the essence of being

a "magnetic person?"

The answer to this is equivalent

to the enlightenment

as a top executive.

(98)

The enlightenment of

management spans from

"how to manage a country"

to "how to make

the Earth prosperous."

Contemplate on the world

you will leave behind.

Aim for the twilight years

in which you can say,

"It was a good life."

Afterword and Commentary

I wrote down essential phrases on work that came to my mind.

They cover guiding principles for all who are working, from new employees to CEOs.

I hope that this book will provide insight into the attitude you should have toward your work and the important mindset for those in managerial and executive positions.

Ryuho Okawa
Master & CEO of Happy Science Group
December 12, 2022

ABOUT THE AUTHOR

Founder and CEO of Happy Science Group.

Ryuho Okawa was born on July 7th 1956, in Tokushima, Japan. After graduating from the University of Tokyo with a law degree, he joined a Tokyo-based trading house. While working at its New York headquarters, he studied international finance at the Graduate Center of the City University of New York. In 1981, he attained Great Enlightenment and became aware that he is El Cantare with a mission to bring salvation to all humankind.

In 1986, he established Happy Science. It now has members in 168 countries across the world, with more than 700 branches and temples as well as 10,000 missionary houses around the world.

He has given over 3,500 lectures (of which more than 150 are in English) and published over 3,100 books (of which more than 600 are Spiritual Interview Series), and many of which are translated into 41 languages. Along with *The Laws of the Sun* and *The Laws of Hell*, many of the books have become best sellers or million sellers. To date, Happy Science has produced 27 movies under the supervision of Okawa. He has given the original story and concept and is also the Executive Producer. He has also composed music and written lyrics of over 450 pieces.

Moreover, he is the Founder of Happy Science University and Happy Science Academy (Junior and Senior High School), Founder and President of the Happiness Realization Party, Founder and Honorary Headmaster of Happy Science Institute of Government and Management, Founder of IRH Press Co., Ltd., and the Chairperson of NEW STAR PRODUCTION Co., Ltd. and ARI Production Co., Ltd.

BOOKS BY RYUHO OKAWA

Words of Wisdom Series

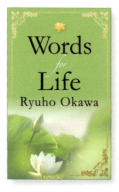

Words for Life

Paperback • 136 pages • $15.95
ISBN: 979-8-88727-089-7 (Mar. 16, 2023)

Ryuho Okawa has written over 3,100 books on various topics. To help readers find the teachings that are beneficial for them out of the extensive teachings, the author has written 100 phrases and put them together in this book. Inside you will find words of wisdom that will help you improve your mindset and lead you to live a meaningful and happy life.

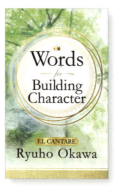

Words for Building Character

Paperback • 140 pages • $15.95
ISBN: 979-8-88737-091-0 (Jun. 21, 2023)

As you read this book, you will discover the wisdom to build a noble character through various life experiences. When your life comes to an end, what you can bring with you to the other world is, in Buddhism terms, enlightenment, and in other words, it is the character that you build in this lifetime. If you can read, relish, and truly understand the meaning of these religious phrases, you will be able to attain happiness that transcends this world and the next.

Words to Read in Times of Illness

Paperback • 136 pages • $15.95
ISBN: 978-1-958655-07-8 (Sep. 15, 2023)

Ryuho Okawa's 100 Healing Messages of Light with the spiritual truths to comfort the souls of those going through any illness. Okawa indicates that when we are ill, it is an ideal time for us to recall and contemplate recent and past events, as well as our relationship with people around us. It is a chance for us to take inventory of our emotions and thoughts buried during our busy everyday life.

Success Books

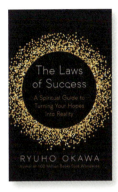

The Laws of Success

A Spiritual Guide to Turning
Your Hopes Into Reality

Paperback • 208 pages • $15.95
ISBN: 978-1-942125-15-0 (Mar. 15, 2017)

The Laws of Success offers 8 spiritual principles that, when put to practice in our day-to-day life, will help us attain lasting success. The timeless wisdom and practical steps that Ryuho Okawa offers will guide us through any difficulties and problems we may face in life, and serve as guiding principles for living a positive, constructive, and meaningful life.

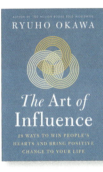

The Art of Influence

28 Ways to Win People's Hearts and Bring Positive
Change to Your Life

Paperback • 264 pages • $15.95
ISBN: 978-1-942125-48-8 (Jan. 15, 2019)

Ryuho Okawa answers to 28 questions he received from people who are aspiring to achieve greater success in life. At times of trouble, setback, or stress, these pages will offer you the inspirations you need at that very moment and open a new avenue for greater success in life. The practiced wisdom that Okawa offers in this book will enrich and fill your heart with motivation, inspiration, and encouragement.

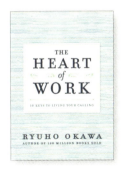

The Heart of Work

10 Keys to Living Your Calling

Paperback • 176 pages • $12.95
ISBN: 978-1-942125-03-7 (Aug. 1, 2016)

In this book, Ryuho Okawa shares 10 key philosophies and goals to live by to guide us through our work lives and triumphantly live our calling. There are key principles that will help you get to the heart of work, manage your time well, prioritize your work, live with long health and vitality, achieve growth, and more.

El Cantare Trilogy

The Laws Series is an annual volume of books that are comprised of Ryuho Okawa's lectures that function as universal guidance to all people. They are of various topics that were given in accordance with the changes that each year brings. *The Laws of the Sun*, the first publication of the laws series and a series written through automatic writing, ranked in the annual best-selling list in Japan in 1994. Since, the laws series' titles have ranked in the annual best-selling list every year for more than two decades, setting socio-cultural trends in Japan and around the world.

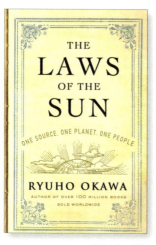

The Laws of the Sun

One Source, One Planet, One People

Paperback • 288 pages • $15.95
ISBN: 978-1-942125-43-3 (Oct. 15, 2018)

IMAGINE IF YOU COULD ASK GOD why He created this world and what spiritual laws He used to shape us—and everything around us. If we could understand His designs and intentions, we could discover what our goals in life should be and whether our actions move us closer to those goals or farther away.

At a young age, a spiritual calling prompted Ryuho Okawa to outline what he innately understood to be universal truths for all humankind. In *The Laws of the Sun*, Okawa outlines these laws of the universe and provides a road map for living one's life with greater purpose and meaning. In this powerful book, Ryuho Okawa reveals the transcendent nature of consciousness and the secrets of our multidimensional universe and our place in it. By understanding the different stages of love and following the Buddhist Eightfold Path, he believes we can speed up our eternal process of development. *The Laws of the Sun* shows the way to realize true happiness—a happiness that continues from this world through the other.

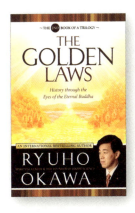

The Golden Laws

History through the Eyes of
the Eternal Buddha

E-book • 204 pages • $13.99
ISBN: 978-1-941779-82-8 (Sep. 24, 2015)

Throughout history, Great Guiding Spirits have been present on Earth in both the East and the West at crucial points in human history to further our spiritual development. *The Golden Laws* reveals how Divine Plan has been unfolding on Earth, and outlines 5,000 years of the secret history of humankind. Once we understand the true course of history, through past, present and into the future, we cannot help but become aware of the significance of our spiritual mission in the present age.

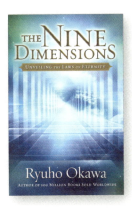

The Nine Dimensions

Unveiling the Laws of Eternity

Paperback • 168 pages • $15.95
ISBN: 978-0-982698-56-3 (Feb. 16, 2012)

This book is a window into the mind of our loving God, who designed this world and the vast, wondrous world of our afterlife as a school with many levels through which our souls learn and grow. When the religions and cultures of the world discover the truth of their common spiritual origin, they will be inspired to accept their differences, come together under faith in God, and build an era of harmony and peaceful progress on Earth.

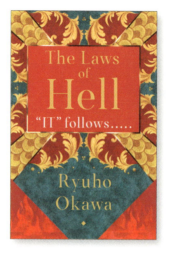

The Laws of Hell

"IT" follows.....

Paperback • 264 pages • $17.95
ISBN: 978-1-958655-04-7 (May 1, 2023)

Whether you believe it or not, the Spirit World and hell do exist. Currently, the Earth's population has exceeded 8 billion, and unfortunately, 1 in 2 people are falling to hell.

This book is a must-read at a time like this since more and more people are unknowingly heading to hell; the truth is, new areas of hell are being created, such as 'internet hell' and 'hell on earth.' Also, due to the widespread materialism, there is a sharp rise in the earthbound spirits wandering around Earth because they have no clue about the Spirit World.

To stop hell from spreading and to save the souls of all human beings, Ryuho Okawa has compiled vital teachings in this book. This publication marks his 3,100th book and is the one and only comprehensive Truth about the modern hell.

New Books

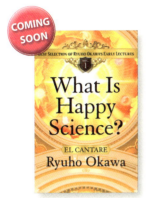

What Is Happy Science?

Best Selection of Ryuho Okawa's Early Lectures (Volume 1)

Paperback • 256 pages • $17.95
ISBN: 978-1-942125-99-0 (Aug. 25, 2023)

The Best Selection series is a collection of Ryuho Okawa's passionate lectures during the ages of 32 to 33 that reveal the mission and goal of Happy Science. This book contains the eternal Truth, including the meaning of life, the secret of the mind, the true meaning of love, the mystery of the universe, and how to end hatred and world conflicts.

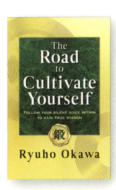

The Road to Cultivate Yourself

Follow Your Silent Voice Within to Gain True Wisdom

Paperback • 256 pages • $17.95
ISBN: 978-1-958655-05-4 (Jun. 22, 2023)

What is the ideal way of living when chaos and destruction are accelerated?
This book offers unchanging Truth in the ever-changing world, such as the secrets to become more aware about the spiritual self and how to increase intellectual productivity amidst the rapid changes of the modern age. It is packed with Ryuho Okawa's crystallized wisdom of life.

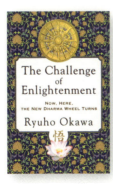

The Challenge of Enlightenment

Now, Here, the New Dharma Wheel Turns

Paperback • 380 pages • $17.95
ISBN: 978-1-942125-92-1 (Dec. 20, 2022)

Buddha's teachings, a reflection of his eternal wisdom, are like a bamboo pole used to change the course of your boat in the rapid stream of the great river called life. By reading this book, your mind becomes clearer, learns to savor inner peace, and it will empower you to make profound life improvements.

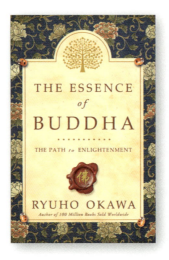

The Essence of Buddha

The Path to Enlightenment

Paperback • 208 pages • $14.95
ISBN: 978-1-942125-06-8 (Oct.1, 2016)

In this book, Ryuho Okawa imparts in simple and accessible language his wisdom about the essence of Shakyamuni Buddha's philosophy of life and enlightenment–teachings that have been inspiring people all over the world for over 2,500 years. By offering a new perspective on core Buddhist thoughts that have long been cloaked in mystique, Okawa brings these teachings to life for modern people. *The Essence of Buddha* distills a way of life that anyone can practice to achieve a life of self-growth, compassionate living, and true happiness.

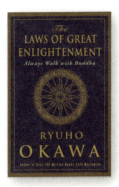

The Laws of Great Enlightenment

Always Walk with Buddha

Paperback • 232 pages • $17.95
ISBN: 978-1-942125-62-4 (Nov. 7, 2019)

Constant self-blame for mistakes, setbacks, or failures and feelings of unforgivingness toward others are hard to overcome. Through the power of enlightenment we can learn to forgive ourselves and others, overcome life's problems, and courageously create a brighter future ourselves. *The Laws of Great Enlightenment* addresses the core problems of life that people often struggle with and offers advice on how to overcome them based on spiritual truths.

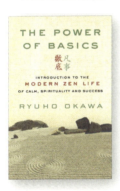

The Power of Basics

Introduction to Modern Zen Life of Calm, Spirituality and Success

Paperback • 232 pages • $16.95
ISBN:978-1-942125-75-4 (Nov. 15, 2020)

The power of basics is a necessary asset to excel at any kind of work. It is the power to meticulously pursue tasks with a quiet Zen mindset. If you master this power of basics, you can achieve new levels of productivity regardless of your profession, and attain new heights of success and happiness. This book also describes the essence of an intellectual life, thereby reviving the true spirit of Zen in the modern age.

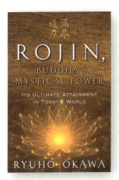

Rojin, Buddha's Mystical Power

Its Ultimate Attainment in Today's World

Paperback • 224 pages • $16.95
ISBN: 978-1-942125-82-2 (Sep. 24, 2021)

In this book, Ryuho Okawa has redefined the traditional Buddhist term *Rojin* and explained that in modern society it means the following: the ability for individuals with great spiritual powers to live in the world as people with common sense while using their abilities to the optimal level. This book will unravel the mystery of the mind and lead you to the path to enlightenment.

Other Recommended Titles

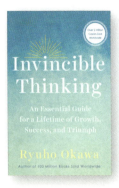

Invincible Thinking

An Essential Guide for a Lifetime of Growth, Success, and Triumph

Hardcover • 208 pages • $16.95
ISBN: 978-1-942125-25-9 (Sep. 5, 2017)

In this book, Ryuho Okawa lays out the principles of invincible thinking that will allow us to achieve long-lasting triumph. This powerful and unique philosophy is not only about becoming successful or achieving our goal in life, but also about building the foundation of life that becomes the basis of our life-long, lasting success and happiness.

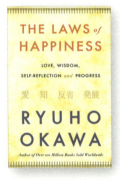

The Laws of Happiness

Love, Wisdom, Self-Reflection and Progress

Paperback • 264 pages • $16.95
ISBN: 978-1-942125-70-9 (Aug. 28, 2020)

Happiness is not found outside us; it is found within us. It is in how we think, how we look at our lives, and how we devote our hearts to the work we do. Discover how the Fourfold Path of Love, Wisdom, Self-Reflection and Progress create a life of sustainable happiness.

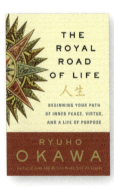

The Royal Road of Life

Beginning Your Path of Inner Peace, Virtue, and a Life of Purpose

Paperback • 224 pages • $16.95
ISBN: 978-1-942125-53-2 (Jan. 15, 2020)

With over 30 years of lectures and teachings spanning diverse topics of faith, self-growth, leadership (and more), Ryuho Okawa presents the profound eastern wisdom that he has cultivated on his approach to life. *The Royal Road of Life* illuminates a path to becoming a person of virtue, whose character and depth will move and inspire others towards the same meaningful destination.

The Ten Principles from El Cantare Volume I
Ryuho Okawa's First Lectures on His Basic Teachings

The Ten Principles from El Cantare Volume II
Ryuho Okawa's First Lectures on His Wish to Save the World

Twiceborn
My Early Thoughts that Revealed My True Mission

Developmental Stages of Love - The Original Theory
Philosophy of Love in My Youth

The Miracle of Meditation
Opening Your Life to Peace, Joy and the Power Within

The True Eightfold Path
Guideposts for Self-Innovation

The Challenge of the Mind
An Essential Guide to Buddha's Teachings:
Zen, Karma and Enlightenment

The Rebirth of Buddha
My Eternal Disciples, Hear My Words

The Strong Mind
The Art of Building the Inner Strength
to Overcome Life's Difficulties

For a complete list of books, visit okawabooks.com

WHO IS EL CANTARE?

El Cantare means "the Light of the Earth." He is the Supreme God of the Earth who has been guiding humankind since the beginning of Genesis, and He is the Creator of the universe. He is whom Jesus called Father and Muhammad called Allah, and is *Ame-no-Mioya-Gami*, Japanese Father God. Different parts of El Cantare's core consciousness have descended to Earth in the past, once as Alpha and another as Elohim. His branch spirits, such as Shakyamuni Buddha and Hermes, have descended to Earth many times and helped to flourish many civilizations. To unite various religions and to integrate various fields of study in order to build a new civilization on Earth, a part of the core consciousness has descended to Earth as Master Ryuho Okawa.

Alpha is a part of the core consciousness of El Cantare who descended to Earth around 330 million years ago. Alpha preached Earth's Truths to harmonize and unify Earth-born humans and space people who came from other planets.

Elohim is a part of the core consciousness of El Cantare who descended to Earth around 150 million years ago. He gave wisdom, mainly on the differences of light and darkness, good and evil.

Ame-no-Mioya-Gami (Japanese Father God) is the Creator God and the Father God who appears in the ancient literature, *Hotsuma Tsutae*. It is believed that He descended on the foothills of Mt. Fuji about 30,000 years ago and built the Fuji dynasty, which is the root of the Japanese civilization. With justice as the central pillar, Ame-no-Mioya-Gami's teachings spread to ancient civilizations of other countries in the world.

Shakyamuni Buddha was born as a prince into the Shakya Clan in India around 2,600 years ago. When he was 29 years old, he renounced the world and sought enlightenment. He later attained Great Enlightenment and founded Buddhism.

Hermes is one of the 12 Olympian gods in Greek mythology, but the spiritual Truth is that he taught the teachings of love and progress around 4,300 years ago that became the origin of the current Western civilization. He is a hero that truly existed.

Ophealis was born in Greece around 6,500 years ago and was the leader who took an expedition to as far as Egypt. He is the God of miracles, prosperity, and arts, and is known as Osiris in the Egyptian mythology.

Rient Arl Croud was born as a king of the ancient Incan Empire around 7,000 years ago and taught about the mysteries of the mind. In the heavenly world, he is responsible for the interactions that take place between various planets.

Thoth was an almighty leader who built the golden age of the Atlantic civilization around 12,000 years ago. In the Egyptian mythology, he is known as God Thoth.

Ra Mu was a leader who built the golden age of the civilization of Mu around 17,000 years ago. As a religious leader and a politician, he ruled by uniting religion and politics.

ABOUT HAPPY SCIENCE

Happy Science is a religious group founded on the faith in El Cantare who is the God of the Earth, and the Creator of the universe. The essence of human beings is the soul that was created by God, and we all are children of God. God is our true parent, so in our souls we have a fundamental desire to "believe in God, love God, and get closer to God." And, we can get closer to God by living with God's Will as our own. In Happy Science, we call this the "Exploration of Right Mind." More specifically, it means to practice the Fourfold Path, which consists of "Love, Wisdom, Self-Reflection, and Progress."

Love: Love means "love that gives," or mercy. God hopes for the happiness of all people. Therefore, living with God's Will as our own means to start by practicing "love that gives."

Wisdom: By studying and putting spiritual knowledge into practice, you can cultivate wisdom and become better at resolving problems in life.

Self-Reflection: Once you learn the heart of God and the difference between His mind and yours, you should strive to bring your own mind closer to the mind of God—that process is called self-reflection. Self-reflection also includes meditation and prayer.

Progress: Since God hopes for the happiness of all people, you should also make progress in your love, and make an effort to realize utopia in which everyone in your society, country, and eventually all humankind can become happy.

As we practice this Fourfold Path, our souls will advance toward God step by step. That is when we can attain real happiness—our souls' desire to get closer to God comes true.

In Happy Science, we conduct activities to make ourselves happy through belief in Lord El Cantare, and to spread this faith to the world and bring happiness to all. We welcome you to join our activities!

We hold events and activities to help you practice the Fourfold Path at our branches, temples, missionary centers and missionary houses

Love: We hold various volunteering activities. Our members conduct missionary work together as the greatest practice of love.

Wisdom: We offer our comprehensive books collection, many of which are available online and at Happy Science locations. In addition, we give out numerous opportunities such as seminars or book clubs to learn the Truth.

Self-Reflection: We offer opportunities to polish your mind through self-reflection, meditation, and prayer. There are many cases in which members have experienced improvement in their human relationships by changing their own minds.

Progress: We also offer seminars to enhance your power of influence. Because it is also important to do well at work to make society better, we hold seminars to improve your work and management skills.

"The True Words Spoken By Buddha"

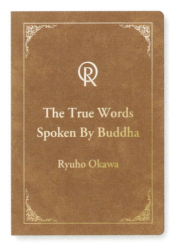

The True Words Spoken By Buddha is an English sutra given directly from the spirit of Shakyamuni Buddha, who is a part of Master Ryuho Okawa's subconscious. The words in this sutra are not of a mere human being but are the words of God or Buddha sent directly from the ninth dimension, which is the highest realm of the Earth's Spirit World.

The True Words Spoken By Buddha is an essential sutra for us to connect and live with God or Buddha's Will as our own.

MEMBERSHIPS

MEMBERSHIP

If you would like to know more about Happy Science, please consider becoming a member. Those who pledge to believe in Lord El Cantare and wish to learn more can join us.

When you become a member, you will receive the following sutra books: *The True Words Spoken By Buddha*, *Prayer to the Lord* and *Prayer to Guardian and Guiding Spirits*.

DEVOTEE MEMBER

If you would like to learn the teachings of Happy Science and walk the path of faith, become a Devotee member who pledges devotion to the Three Treasures, which are Buddha, Dharma, and Sangha. Buddha refers to Lord El Cantare, Master Ryuho Okawa. Dharma refers to Master Ryuho Okawa's teachings. Sangha refers to Happy Science. Devoting to the Three Treasures will let your Buddha-nature shine, and you will enter the path to attain true freedom of the mind.

Becoming a devotee means you become Buddha's disciple. You will discipline your mind and act to bring happiness to society.

✉ EMAIL or ☏ PHONE CALL
Please see the contact information page.

☏ ONLINE | member.happy-science.org/signup/ |

CONTACT INFORMATION

Happy Science is a worldwide organization with branches and temples around the globe. For a comprehensive list, visit the worldwide directory at happy-science.org. The following are some of our main Happy Science locations:

UNITED STATES AND CANADA

New York
79 Franklin St., New York, NY 10013, USA
Phone: 1-212-343-7972
Fax: 1-212-343-7973
Email: ny@happy-science.org
Website: happyscience-usa.org

New Jersey
66 Hudson St., #2R, Hoboken, NJ 07030, USA
Phone: 1-201-313-0127
Email: nj@happy-science.org
Website: happyscience-usa.org

Chicago
2300 Barrington Rd., Suite #400,
Hoffman Estates, IL 60169, USA
Phone: 1-630-937-3077
Email: chicago@happy-science.org
Website: happyscience-usa.org

Florida
5208 8th St., Zephyrhills, FL 33542, USA
Phone: 1-813-715-0000
Fax: 1-813-715-0010
Email: florida@happy-science.org
Website: happyscience-usa.org

Atlanta
1874 Piedmont Ave., NE Suite 360-C
Atlanta, GA 30324, USA
Phone: 1-404-892-7770
Email: atlanta@happy-science.org
Website: happyscience-usa.org

San Francisco
525 Clinton St.
Redwood City, CA 94062, USA
Phone & Fax: 1-650-363-2777
Email: sf@happy-science.org
Website: happyscience-usa.org

Los Angeles
1590 E. Del Mar Blvd., Pasadena, CA
91106, USA
Phone: 1-626-395-7775
Fax: 1-626-395-7776
Email: la@happy-science.org
Website: happyscience-usa.org

Orange County
16541 Gothard St. Suite 104
Huntington Beach, CA 92647
Phone: 1-714-659-1501
Email: oc@happy-science.org
Website: happyscience-usa.org

San Diego
7841 Balboa Ave. Suite #202
San Diego, CA 92111, USA
Phone: 1-626-395-7775
Fax: 1-626-395-7776
E-mail: sandiego@happy-science.org
Website: happyscience-usa.org

Hawaii
Phone: 1-808-591-9772
Fax: 1-808-591-9776
Email: hi@happy-science.org
Website: happyscience-usa.org

Kauai
3343 Kanakolu Street, Suite 5
Lihue, HI 96766, USA
Phone: 1-808-822-7007
Fax: 1-808-822-6007
Email: kauai-hi@happy-science.org
Website: happyscience-usa.org

Toronto

845 The Queensway
Etobicoke, ON M8Z 1N6, Canada
Phone: 1-416-901-3747
Email: toronto@happy-science.org
Website: happy-science.ca

Vancouver

#201-2607 East 49th Avenue,
Vancouver, BC, V5S 1J9, Canada
Phone: 1-604-437-7735
Fax: 1-604-437-7764
Email: vancouver@happy-science.org
Website: happy-science.ca

INTERNATIONAL

Tokyo

1-6-7 Togoshi, Shinagawa,
Tokyo, 142-0041, Japan
Phone: 81-3-6384-5770
Fax: 81-3-6384-5776
Email: tokyo@happy-science.org
Website: happy-science.org

London

3 Margaret St.
London, W1W 8RE United Kingdom
Phone: 44-20-7323-9255
Fax: 44-20-7323-9344
Email: eu@happy-science.org
Website: www.happyscience-uk.org

Sydney

516 Pacific Highway, Lane Cove North,
2066 NSW, Australia
Phone: 61-2-9411-2877
Fax: 61-2-9411-2822
Email: sydney@happy-science.org

Sao Paulo

Rua. Domingos de Morais 1154,
Vila Mariana, Sao Paulo SP
CEP 04010-100, Brazil
Phone: 55-11-5088-3800
Email: sp@happy-science.org
Website: happyscience.com.br

Jundiai

Rua Congo, 447, Jd. Bonfiglioli
Jundiai-CEP, 13207-340, Brazil
Phone: 55-11-4587-5952
Email: jundiai@happy-science.org

Seoul

74, Sadang-ro 27-gil,
Dongjak-gu, Seoul, Korea
Phone: 82-2-3478-8777
Fax: 82-2-3478-9777
Email: korea@happy-science.org

Taipei

No. 89, Lane 155, Dunhua N. Road,
Songshan District, Taipei City 105, Taiwan
Phone: 886-2-2719-9377
Fax: 886-2-2719-5570
Email: taiwan@happy-science.org

Taichung

No. 146, Minzu Rd., Central Dist.,
Taichung City 400001, Taiwan
Phone: 886-4-22233777
Email: taichung@happy-science.org

Kuala Lumpur

No 22A, Block 2, Jalil Link Jalan Jalil
Jaya 2, Bukit Jalil 57000,
Kuala Lumpur, Malaysia
Phone: 60-3-8998-7877
Fax: 60-3-8998-7977
Email: malaysia@happy-science.org
Website: happyscience.org.my

Kathmandu

Kathmandu Metropolitan City,
Ward No. 15, Ring Road, Kimdol,
Sitapaila Kathmandu, Nepal
Phone: 977-1-537-2931
Email: nepal@happy-science.org

Kampala

Plot 877 Rubaga Road, Kampala
P.O. Box 34130 Kampala, UGANDA
Email: uganda@happy-science.org

The Happiness Realization Party (HRP) was founded in May 2009 by Master Ryuho Okawa as part of the Happy Science Group. HRP strives to improve the Japanese society, based on three basic political principles of "freedom, democracy, and faith," and let Japan promote individual and public happiness from Asia to the world as a leader nation.

1) Diplomacy and Security: Protecting Freedom, Democracy, and Faith of Japan and the World from China's Totalitarianism

Japan's current defense system is insufficient against China's expanding hegemony and the threat of North Korea's nuclear missiles. Japan, as the leader of Asia, must strengthen its defense power and promote strategic diplomacy together with the nations which share the values of freedom, democracy, and faith. Further, HRP aims to realize world peace under the leadership of Japan, the nation with the spirit of religious tolerance.

2) Economy: Early economic recovery through utilizing the "wisdom of the private sector"

Economy has been damaged severely by the novel coronavirus originated in China. Many companies have been forced into bankruptcy or out of business. What is needed for economic recovery now is not subsidies and regulations by the government, but policies which can utilize the "wisdom of the private sector."

For more information, visit en.hr-party.jp